Authority in Crisis?
An Anglican Response

AUTHORITY IN CRISIS?

An Anglican Response

—

ROBERT RUNCIE
Archbishop of Canterbury

SCM PRESS LTD

British Library Cataloguing in Publication Data

Runcie, Robert, *1921–*
Authority in crisis : an Anglican response.
1. Authority – Christian viewpoints
I. Title
261

ISBN 0–334–01882–X

First published 1988
by SCM Press Ltd
26 – 30 Tottenham Road, London N1 4BZ

Phototypeset by Input Typesetting Ltd, London
and printed in Great Britain by
Richard Clay Ltd, Bungay, Suffolk

Contents

Preface

In the matter of writing books latter-day Archbishops look wistfully at their more leisured predecessors, who were enviably less constrained by the tyranny of the diary and the pace of contemporary life. Even so, it may be that their most reflective books were produced before reaching archiepiscopal office. In these lectures on authority, at any rate, the reader will find the impressions of a practitioner rather than the systematics of an academic theologian. Perhaps this is no bad thing. Bishops do have to exercise authority in their dioceses. They do have to come to decisions in concert with clergy and laity in Synods. They will be attending the forthcoming Lambeth Conference at which the question of authority underlies the particularities of a detailed agenda, and they will have to take decisions of lasting consequence for the future of the Communion. Nor is there a lack of more professional theological reflection available. I think particularly of the book of essays presented to Bishop Howe, edited by Stephen Sykes *Authority in the Anglican Communion*.

The three pieces in this book are therefore an example of an Archbishop thinking on his feet in the face of authority in crisis in the secular world and the Anglican Communion. Not, however, unaided. I want to record my gratitude for important insights gained from theologians such as Stephen Sykes and Nicholas Lash, friends from my cell, Lambeth staff and, most importantly, the experience of other Christians as refracted through our ecumenical dialogues.

The three pieces before you were occasioned in January 1988 by Trinity Institute, New York. I record my gratitude to Trinity Institute for inviting me to give two lectures in New York and San Francisco on the subjects of the two main chapters. I am also grateful that they have been so helpful over the publication of the lectures this side of the Atlantic. The first chapter is my sermon at the opening eucharist and therefore has a more homiletic character.

I have been persuaded to agree to publish these lectures in the hope that the questions raised will provoke some constructive discussion on the eve of the Lambeth Conference. I am aware of many of their deficiencies, but would ask for them to be read with a remembrance that they were delivered as a pair of lectures with an audience meeting afterwards in 'workshops' to discuss, criticize and respond to my initial contributions. The titles given me were all-embracing and the only way to cover the ground was to move assertively from point to point without overmuch detailed argument.

I have made some relatively minor changes in respect of English publication, but an awareness of their North American context will assist understanding. In the United States the title originally given to me for what is now Chapter 3 was '*The* Anglican Response'. But it is usually easier to recognize a problem than solve it so definitively. In any case Archbishops of Canterbury should not get in the habit of writing authoritatively *motu proprio*. In the knowledge that most Anglicans know this well enough I offer these lectures as a contribution to the debate.

✠ ROBERT CANTUAR:

– 1 –

The Authority of the Servant

'Whoever would be great among you must be your servant, and whoever would be first among you must be slave of all' (Mark 10.43.44).

It is one of the strange victories of Jesus Christ that what he thought to be a paradox has become in our age a platitude. Everyone now wants to be thought of as rendering a service. Nothing is more esteemed than the business of serving our fellow men and women. It is a commonly accepted sign of greatness.

But it was not so in the time of Jesus Christ. Greatness depended largely upon accident of birth. If you were born into the nobility or ruling class you were, whatever your moral qualities or lack of them, a great man. (Great women had scarcely then been invented.) If you were born outside this charmed circle, it did not matter much how hard you worked or how wealthy you became – *Greatness* would always elude you. For in the societies of ancient Greece, ancient Rome and Palestine, it would have sounded absurd to refer to a farmer, a merchant or a secretary as 'a great man'. It would have sounded even more absurd then to say that a servant might be great. We can surely trust that the words which I began by quoting were uttered by Jesus: they would have sounded so odd, so paradoxical that they must have remained a puzzle in the minds of the disciples.

Yet the puzzle now seems much less perplexing. In our age – and perhaps in the United States more plainly than in any other country – greatness is not associated with birth into a certain family or class but by *service* to the nation or the world. Even in Britain the English aristocrat loses status in society if he does not prove himself of service, even if it is simply by opening his house to the public. The respect that is given to people is proportionate to their usefulness in the world, their contribution to the good of society; put simply, their *service*. Every presidential candidate seeking the respect, favour and votes of the electorate wants to be seen as the servant of the nation. Every institution in society seeks respect because of the service which it performs. In 1987 the secret police force of the Soviet Union – the KGB – celebrated (if that's the right word) its seventieth anniversary. The occasion was marked by various ceremonies and publications. Amongst the statements which came out of the Soviet Union was one which said, 'The KGB has always been the *servant* of the Soviet working class.' A strange idea, you might think, but it just shows how universal is the assent of our age to the teaching of Jesus that it is only in the role of servant that greatness resides.

It is only the role of the servant that makes a man or an institution great and entitles that man or that institution to respect, admiration and even obedience. Yes, this is a sort of victory for the teaching of Jesus, as I said at the beginning. But Jesus was not teaching us how to win respect in the world but how we should live as the Lord's disciples.

If we present ourselves as servants and win the world's respect, this has its own dangers. For the world's respect brings its own reward – of influence, prestige, even power. That prospect may corrupt even sincere and generous Christian motives. We cannot afford any longer to exempt the role of the servant from critical analysis.

We have heard much talk in recent years of the 'servant church'. No description could be more in keeping with the teaching of Jesus, but 'the servant church' is still under judgment. It is required to 'give an account of its stewardship'. In an age in which any form of useful activity is called service, and in which – at least in the United Kingdom – the term 'service industries' is commonly used of any non-manufacturing business, then the content and character of the role of the servant needs close examination.

For the Christian, such an examination must begin with the person of Jesus Christ. St Paul, writing to the Philippians, tells us that 'Jesus Christ, though he was in the form of God, did not count equality with God a thing to be grasped, but emptied himself, taking the form of a servant, being born in the likeness of men.' Jesus Christ is our measure of service. St Paul goes on to say that, 'being found in human form, Jesus humbled Himself.' To be a servant is not enough. Humility is called for, too. And that does not necessarily win respect in the world. The story is told of a small boy who was sent to his school's Headmaster because his teacher found him so consistently cocky and impertinent. The Headmaster urged the small boy to adopt humility. So he did, for a bit; then he lapsed into his old self. 'So how about the humility, then?' asked the Head. 'I *was* humble for a fortnight,' the boy said, 'but nobody noticed.' That's the trouble with the humble servant as far as the world is concerned. Nobody would notice him. I am reminded of my own school report. 'With a little discouragement he will do better.'

The school of experience teaches us a good deal about humility. Benjamin Franklin once said: 'After crosses and losses, men grow humbler and wiser.' But it would be a sad thing if it was only towards the end of our lives – and especially only if we had experienced more than our fair share of suffering – that this sort of humility was achieved. It can be achieved by living in Christ. His clues to this way of living are contained in his many parables in which servants – humble servants – appear.

Frequently, the servants in the parables are given great responsibilities. Think of the parable of the talents where the man going on the journey entrusts his property to his servants. Or think of the authority given to the servants sent to collect the rent in the parable of the wicked husbandmen. Frequently the servants have themselves to exercise stewardship. The servants of the parables are not obsequious or servile. Nor are they expected to render blind, unthinking obedience. The servant who buries his talent in the ground is not commended.

The other noticeable thing in the parables is the way in which the stewards have responsibilities for their fellow servants. The steward is accountable *to* his master *for* his fellow servants; he is to exercise *among* his fellow servants the will of *his master*. These two things have to be held in tension. The steward is no 'good and faithful servant' if he bases his authority exclusively on the appreciation by his fellow servants of what he does for them. If he does so, he may find himself 'a rebellious servant' in his master's eyes. The faithful steward exercises his responsibility by *both* an attentive service to the expressed wishes and needs of his fellow servants *and* an attentive study of, and obedience to, his master's will. *In that we see a parable of the Christian life.*

And it is also a parable of the servant church. Yes, the church must heed Christ's teaching that there is no authority except that which belongs to the role of the servant. It should scrutinize its performance in that role to see how it might be extended and for those elements of self-advertisement or empire-building which should be eradicated from it. It should ensure that in its service to society its people are not fumbling amateurs but 'as wise as serpents' as well as 'harmless as doves'. But nothing would be more tragic than if, in taking seriously Christ's teaching about the authority of service, the church should find itself in unwitting rebellion against the authority of Christ himself.

Our obedience to his will which is also the will of his Father is expressed in the celebration of the Eucharist. In the self-forgetfulness of prayer and worship the authority of God is made known to us in the face of Jesus Christ, not only drawing from us loving service but making us into his character and likeness.

May it ever be our resolve 'to keep his holy will ever before us'; not to run before every wind of political, economic or sociological doctrine to which we are exposed, but to look 'unto Jesus, the author and perfecter of our faith'. And in doing this we must avoid that instinct to go for those decisions and policies which are most likely to justify in the eyes of the world our claim to be the 'servant church', and so to bestow upon ourselves a respect and popularity which our Lord and Saviour did not himself seek. What we need to do is to set our minds on those things which are 'well pleasing in *his* sight' who is the Master Servant of us all.

The sharpest concluding sentence of a New Testament book is: 'Little children keep yourselves from idols'. There are plenty of idols today which cry out for our service, but to him first must be our service and loyalty, our respect and gratitude and love.

– 2 –

Authority in Crisis?

I want to go on to reflect, as broadly as possible, upon
the theme of 'Authority in Crisis?' You will have noticed
how the phrase has a question-mark at the end. That
question-mark is essential to my argument. Let me tell
you why.

Those of us whose youth was dominated by the need
to get rid of one particular evil from the world – the evil
of Hitler's Fascism – had certain notions deeply imprinted
upon our minds. The experience of those years dispelled
for ever the belief that authority of the state is necessarily
self-authenticating, and has an intrinsic right to be
believed and followed. The unthinkingly obedient person
may all the time be like the concentration-camp officials
whose defence was that they were acting under orders.
That is no sort of model for Christian obedience to God.
We need authority, of course, but it is fatal not to be
ready to criticize it. We all have a duty to think of
ourselves. Even Cardinal Newman, after the declaration
of papal infallibility, once said: 'if I were to bring religion
into after-dinner speaking – a custom which I do not

recommend – I would drink a toast to the Pope certainly, but to conscience *first.*'

And a second deeply embedded notion from wartime days was a slogan 'Careless talk costs lives.' We need to be aware that the way we talk about crisis can itself generate crisis – to keep saying things are going badly wrong can make things go worse. Fear feeds on fear. Defeatism ensures defeat. We must be on our guard against self-fulfilling prophecy, which produces the very problem that it is afraid of. So let us cherish the question-mark in the title under discussion: let us take a sober, but not a gloomy, view and look at the facts.

The collapse of authority?

A few years ago it would have seemed realistic to talk about the collapse of authority. Rebellion thrived in the home and on the campus, in church and state. At that time authority was seen as the enemy of personal freedom and of individual fulfilment. It stood in the way of personal integrity and authenticity, and so far from being necessarily wise and benevolent it was popularly thought to be unintelligent if not inhuman. Still today authority has a bad press: it is assumed by many to be *ipso facto* oppressive. So, as an Archbishop of Canterbury is only too well aware, the people that interest the media are the rebels, not the conformists: the nun who leaves her community, the priest who resigns his orders. The popular presumption is that integrity belongs to the voice of protest, and institutional authority is inflexible and unbending.

In this questioning of authority, participants found that they had some curious companions. Libertarians of the political right stood shoulder to shoulder with anarchists of the far left. They were united in the belief that morals and values were a matter for the individual and the community only had a right to step in when one individual invaded the rights of another – on the principle: 'My freedom to swing my arm ends where my brother's nose begins.' If people choose to smoke pot – so the argument ran – if they engage in bizarre sexual practices, so long as it is done alone, or in company with others so minded, that is their business. Responsive to this mood, legislators attempted to disengage law and morality, crime and sin.

In this situation it was common to treat the pluralist society, not only as a fact of life, but as an unambiguous good. The secular, or neutral, society was to be celebrated because it left us alone in the great supermarket of values to select according to individual taste and fancy – a kind of moral smörgåsbord.

Now, although this rebellion against authority is still associated in the public mind – on both sides of the Atlantic – with the political left, with anti-war protest and the struggle for minority rights, it also emanates just as logically from the free-market liberalism of the right and an emphasis on personal responsibility and dignity. Its strength and coherence lies in shaking off the smothering all-intrusive state.

I remember the recording of the musical *Hair*. The record sleeve gave us the message 'They're anti-war, anti-dishonesty, pro-life, pro-love, pro-sex, pro-joy, pro-colour, pro-fantasy. They see the uptight "rational world" of the older generation as hypocritical, restrictive and ultimately cruel and violent.' And I am reminded of the teacher, quoted by Allan Bloom in his book *The*

Closing of the American Mind who wrote a Ten Commandments for America which began: 'I am the Lord thy God who brought thee out of the house of European tyrants into my own land, America. Relax!' And yet, oddly enough, it has been the revival of free-market individualism which has led to a kind of counter-revolution, so that those who exalt the virtues of standing on one's own feet and making one's way up the ladder to economic success are the very ones who now turn round and call for a return to the old common values.

Authority making a come-back?

The truth is that the situation which confronts us in 1988 is very different. Now we must speak, not only of the crisis of authority but also of its come-back. Throughout the world, and in a variety of different cultures, throughout the world of Islam and throughout the world of Christendom, there is a sharp re-assertion of what are held to be the 'old' values. Economic liberalism seems to be paving the way for moral conservatism, and theological liberalism seems to be giving way to unreconstructed fundamentalism. The New Right seems here to stay.

Why is this? One could, of course, argue that it springs from sheer panic – panic that there no longer seem to be any rational ways left of securing moral consensus in our society. Or it may be that the upheavals and divisions of the 1960s left a power vacuum into which the state and other authorities have stepped. It was de Tocqueville, in the second part of his *Democracy in America*, who made the prophetic point that any search for change leads to social instability, and eventually creates an opportunity for an increase of power by the state.

But let me put forward two more mundane but equally plausible explanations why the need for agreed authority finds greater acceptance today.

(a) Individualism not enough

First, we seem to be discovering that individualism is simply not enough. We cannot be left free simply to scramble up our individual ladders to success in a personal style of life. The real world is not like that. So the unremitting pursuit of the goals of economic liberalism has led to the recent collapse of the money markets and the painful rediscovery of our interdependence: what happens on Wall Street affects what happens on the London market, and what happens in Tokyo affects them both. Mysterious waves of confidence, or lack of confidence, sweep across the world and add or subtract from the value of shares. This interdependence, this inability of any action to be an island, is of course known, and much more painfully, in the Third World as it struggles with its debts and is forced to conform to the requirements of the International Monetary Fund. We wake to the truth that interdependence is not the wild ideal of dreamers but simply the way things are. To misquote that Walter Mitty of our own time, Woody Allen: 'Who needs a dream with a life like ours.'

One could add that it is an important insight of the Green and Animal Rights movements that the somewhat arrogant picture of humans 'subduing' the world should be replaced by a humbler and more respectful vision of our part in the world's ecology. Scientific students of animal behaviour are also complaining of an imperfectly understood Darwinianism on the part of politicians. Biology is made to be all about individual competition for survival. We win by succeeding, by trampling on others, and thus competition is a model for human social behaviour. In fact co-operation is at least as characteristic of biological evolution, though this has not yet percolated into public discussion. Co-operation should be seen for what it is, an essential part of being alive.

We are discovering that the pursuit of individual goals is not enough. If the law is to work, it has to express some principles and prohibitions which are generally held to be right. The law has to rest on a foundation of common convictions and values. Where it does not, not even law seems able to hold back the dire effects of the moral free-for-all. In the House of Commons, Members of Parliament were shown examples recently of what are known as 'video nasties'. They emerged horrified. Something, they said, had to be done, and what had to be done was more than preventing this material being thrust upon those who did not wish to view it. Society had to make clear that this material offended against some agreed notion of what was held to be decent. In the House of Lords a few years ago there was a debate on violence, which I initiated, and in which concern was expressed about the ease with which individuals turn to violence in support of their ends. It was the former Lord Chancellor (Lord Hailsham) who perceived that the problem was only partly within the range of the law and its enforcement. Criminality he saw to be but an outward and visible expression of attitudes which were more widespread. Dealing with violence would have to mean not only tighter legislation and better policing, but a return to a coherent common view of what was acceptable human behaviour, and to a morality grounded in more than self-interest. Individualism is not enough.

(b) The lonely crowd

A second and equally grievous casualty of the pursuit of pure individualism is the loss of personal identity felt in a pluralist free-for-all society. Ironically, but to the Christian predictably, the cultivation of personal fulfilment cannot be achieved on one's own, and people who attempt it are likely to find that, in David Reisman's memorable phrase, they are lost in 'the lonely crowd'. Most people value not only the sense of 'doing their own thing', but also the sense of belonging to a community, of having roots in the past and, having exhausted themselves in endless autonomous personal initiatives, being able to fall back on a shared way of life. When, whether in West Virginia or South Yorkshire, a coal mine is closed and the community built up around it is threatened, why do its members, offered new work in bright new homes in a different part of the country, decline the offer and choose to be workless where they belong rather than employed where they do not belong? It seems that 'to belong' is felt to be as important as 'to be free', that indeed we cannot be truly free unless we belong. Where patterns of life with their shared values and beliefs are eroded, there arises something more than simple nostalgia for the old ways, a perception that we are made for fellowship with one another, rather than for separate living in different groups, each fuelling indignation against the other with no comprehension of a common story.

Thus to talk about authority in 1988 is more complicated than it was in 1968. There is a new recognition that nationally and internationally we belong together, that there is something more to morals and values than the 'do it yourself' enterprises of individualistic liberalism and that, although it is a fact, the pluralist society is not an unambiguous good. We feel the need to go on from pluralism to something more positive. Like T.S. Eliot, we begin to worry about the moral vacuum of the neutral state. So it is not surprising that we are witnessing on an international scale, and across all cultures and religions, a fundamentalist revival of old values and a reassertion of authority. The rebellion against authority seems to have generated the insecurity which leads us to cry to our old enemy: 'Come back, all is forgiven!'

The lessons of the past

In this there is perhaps something to be learned, incidentally, about the pace with which societies can securely emerge from authoritarian rule, a pace which takes cognizance of the sense of corporate identity and therefore allows movement forward without a loss of security, and the resulting bolt back into the safe arms of authoritarianism. It is a question to which the West should be alert as it urges Mr Gorbachev on and on to ever more perfect *perestroika*. If the speed of 'restructuring' is too fast, may there not be a reaction back into the comparative security of the old ways?

The attempt to put the clock back and return to old securities raises the question: 'Can it work?' It is possible for an articulate minority to strike up an alliance with a nostalgic insecure majority and call for a reaffirmation of values. Indeed this is an alliance to which political parties of all shades and in all countries have to pay heed. Silent submerged conservatism can no longer be simply ignored. So parties of the left are having increasingly to root their policies in some appeal to the past, to parts of a tradition which they claim to have ignored. Roots in the past as well as dreams for the future acquire a new significance. The study of history, much neglected I think in the 1960s, says two things about roots. First, it reveals the way in which a civilized people can suddenly sink back into unimaginable barbarism, as happened to the most civilized of Western nations, Germany, under Nazism. Also, the study of history suggests that it is not natural for people to be good, decent, kind to one another. It seems from history that people have to be taught, and heroes and martyrs have to suffer, in the costly pursuit of those ends.

'Absolutes' and their problems

However the silent majority may cry for authority, as they cry to churches for a firm moral line, they may yet decline to take the medicine which authority prescribes. The moral free-for-all simply continues. Firm words are received with enthusiasm, but the moral values of which they speak continue to be neglected. However much you may sharpen the law and encourage authorities to speak out, you will not necessarily affect a change in the patterns of human behaviour, for it takes more than this to reverse or change such patterns. Something other than traditional authority is needed to win hearts and minds. Frustrated authority thus called on but disobeyed is likely to become increasingly isolated, convinced that like Elijah it alone has not bowed the knee to Baal, and become increasingly ineffectual.

It is all very well to speak, as some have, of 'the Tyranny of Subjectivism'. But to suggest a simplistic return to commonly agreed moral 'absolutes' is not really as helpful as it at first sounds. They are not to be had. Even if the human race could universally agree on what is good or evil, right or wrong, we would still be left with the problems which arise when we try to find an agreed application of these insights.

Can the desired authority be made effective? This is only possible if the insights of liberalism, with its emphasis on individual freedom and responsibility, are jettisoned and authoritarian methods introduced. To turn one's back on pluralism and to attempt to re-establish the positive society in the shape of old values could be achieved, but only under an oppressive and totalitarian régime. This is precisely what some of the more strident moralists of the new Right fail to grasp.

The revival of authority and the return to various brands of fundamentalism have been deeply embarrassing to newly minted radicals, and to traditional liberals in both church and state. It has been attractive to believe in the upward progress of the human race out of the bonds of authority into the perfect liberty of individual autonomy. No wonder there is a reaction of pained surprise. Nothing is more necessary than that the movement that has prided itself on its critical ability should itself become self-critical. Authority comes back in unacceptable and indeed frightening forms, because liberals have consistently failed to realize that liberalism can only thrive in a society which holds strong common moral assumptions.

Liberalism seems powerless when those hidden assumptions are exposed and challenged.

Thinking again

There is, then, an urgent need to think positively about authority, to examine its possibilities and to recognize its inevitability – indeed its necessity – in some form. There is a lot of work to be done to get the nature of authority right, and escape from the either/or of radical permissiveness and reactionary authoritarianism. As C.S. Lewis once said, the devil always sends evil into the world in pairs of opposites: if we criticize authoritarianism we get permissiveness, and if we criticize permissiveness we revert to tyrannies. We swing like a pendulum from a 'do as I say' authoritarianism to a 'do it yourself' individualism.

Let me then, in true Anglican (and archiepiscopal) style, attempt to trace a middle way between these bleak alternatives.

(a) Authority and authoritarianism

First, let us acknowledge that some form of authority is necessary to sustain a common life. However much libertarians have been right to stress personal responsibility and individual dignity, human beings are not isolated islands, and if we are to grasp our interdependence with one another, we shall need a framework, a social order, to support and coordinate our common life.

But more than that, more than a mere prop for our weakness, authority can enable us to grow. While Thomas Hobbes argued that strong authority was necessary to impose civilization on fallen man, without which his existence would be 'solitary, poor, nasty, brutish and short' *(Leviathan* 13.62), an Oxford Professor of Jurisprudence, John Finnis, has convincingly argued that it is precisely where man is most successful and flourishing that he most needs authority. Authority, far from being a necessary evil, is a good concerned to channel, harmonize and thus maximize human riches.

> The greater the intelligence and skill of a group's members and the greater their commitment and dedication to common purposes and common good, the more authority and regulation may be required, to enable that group to achieve its common purpose, common good.[1]

Again,

> Intelligence and dedication, skill and commitments . . . multiply the problems of co-ordination, by giving the group more possible orientations, commitments, projects, priorities, and procedures to choose from. And until a particular choice is made, nothing will in fact be done.[2]

While a string quartet can operate by itself, the richer the variety of instrumentalists you assemble for music-making, the greater the need for a conductor to weld all these excellences into an orchestra.

Once we see authority in this enabling way, we are able to see why 'authoritarianism' is the evil it is. False forms of authority do not result in such freedom and

1. John Finnis, *Natural Law and Natural Rights*, Clarendon Press 1980, p. 231.
2. Ibid, p.232.

flourishing; they create an immature form of dependence. But in contrast to that form of immaturity we have to beware of the opposite, but scarcely more mature, independence which equates freedom with the complete absence of control. To go back to the musical analogy, we are content to take our trumpet and play by ourselves in a corner. If we want to develop our musical experience we must advance beyond this immature independence and discover the mature dependence of putting ourselves under the conductor's baton. The good conductor, exerting genuine authority, knows both how to respect the individual gifts of his players and how to co-ordinate those gifts in the common enterprise. St Paul, in describing the varied gifts of the Spirit, modestly omitted to mention his work as leader.

(b) A matter of size

Second, we need to recognize that the nature and size of the enterprise determines the style of authority required to sustain it.

If we are not to be doomed to a sterile choice between individualism and centralism, we need to ask what form of authority is appropriate for the particular enterprise in question. When we talk about 'the common life', we need to ask: 'The common life of what?' When we talk about the common life of the nation, we find ourselves increasingly driven to talk about the common life of this small planet to which the nation belongs, and also of the manifold small groups which belong to the nation. At each level of concern there will be a variety of authorities, appropriate to the activity in question. T.S. Eliot argued that 'the way of life' of a people was fed into, and kept alive by, the flourishing of what he called a 'constellation' of cultures within the nation.[3] The way of life of a nation is richer if it is made up of a number of ways of life within it. The orchestra is not simply the bringing together of individual instrumentalists into a common enterprise but also the bringing together of sub-groups: strings, woodwind, brass, percussion. For each level to flourish, whether we look outwards to the world community or inwards to the fundamental unit of association, the family, it must be coherently organized, not chaotic. And each will work best where, under its own conductor, it has developed a life of its own to bring to the wider community.

The common good is increased where the larger bodies with their own proper authorities make room for lesser bodies to operate with them.

Thus to perceive and respect a variety of authorities does not mean that authority is so dispersed that it ceases to be effective: rather, by keeping within its proper limits the reverse happens. Remote authority is not only felt to be tyrannical; it is notoriously ineffective. Only an authority tailored to weld together and harmonize the purposes of each enterprise has the chance of being effective authority. If authority is to be recognized as creative and not oppressive; if it is to be experienced as liberating rather than constraining: if it is to be capable of harmonizing and promoting variety: if it is perceived as personal and not remote, then we shall have gone at least some way in turning the crisis of our title into an opportunity.

3. T.S. Eliot, *Notes towards the Definition of Culture*, Faber 1948, p. 54.

My analogy here might be the work of the ecologist. We need a creative authority capable of encouraging pluriformity; of preserving the human and social equivalents of marshes, wild flowers and undomesticated, pre-urban fauna. I thought about that when I went to an agricultural show, and they showed me all the achievements of modern argiculture and industry and then took me to an area where wild flowers grew all along the hedges. There was an immense variety and someone turned to me and said: 'It is just like theology: you don't need just tidiness, you need texture too.'

Recapitulation: the argument so far

So far I have deliberately tried to treat this subject of authority in the widest possible context. It seemed best to examine the question from the general standpoint before proceeding to the particular contributions and concerns of Christian faith, and later on of Anglicanism, following (if you like) a Thomist scheme: nature first, then grace.

But I hope that what I have said may have produced resonances with the Christian tradition, and echoes of disputes from Christian history. Be that as it may, there are connections here which now need to be made explicit.

First, let me remind you of my argument, or rather of my description of the crisis in secular authority. I have spoken of Western societies as painfully discovering that a libertarian individualism is no longer enough. But an emotional return to forms of authoritarianism, whether of left or right, is not enough either. Nor will such new authoritarianism work. The clock cannot be put back, however strident the new rhetoric. I then argued for a new style of authority as a good; an understanding of authority as a framework of common values which enables personal talents to be co-ordinated for the good of all: my analogy of the conductor and the orchestra. Such a view of authority depends upon a fresh recognition of human interdependence, of the fact that we belong to each other. I finally suggested that forms of authority which have as their goal the welfare of the whole must deliberately make space for subordinate organs of authority if society is to be healthy and flourish in all its parts. Bearing all this in mind, let us now pay attention to some correspondences as we begin to look at the problem of authority from a specifically Christian perspective.

The inevitability of authority

Christians must start with the inevitability of authority. To believe in God, the ultimate reality, is to believe in the authority of God. To believe in Jesus as the word made flesh is to believe that the man Jesus Christ uniquely communicates the authority of God. To believe that the crucified Jesus lives is to believe that his unique communication of the authority of God continues to be heard. To belong to the church is to believe that this is the locus where that 'Word of God' is authentically preached. We cannot, therefore, avoid the question of authority. The New Testament witnesses constantly to the authority of God as mediated through Jesus, and that this mediation continues in mission to the world within the communion of faith. Twentieth-century Christians are no more left in a free market to make their own faith than were Peter, James and John. Peter, James, John, you and I, are all addressed by the ultimate authority of the

Word of God in Christ Jesus. And, as in the first century, this word does not come to us as lone individuals, but in our human interdependence.

So the question about authority for Christians – as we have already discovered for social scientists and politicians – is not whether we have it, but of what sort it is to be.

The authority of the cross

For the Christian, there can be no answer to the question 'What sort of authority?' which ignores the cross. You will recall that Jesus, in St Mark's Gospel, (10.35ff.) says:

> You know that those who are supposed to rule over the Gentiles lord it over them, and their great men exercise authority over them. But it shall not be so among you; whoever would be great among you must be your servant, and whoever would be first among you must be slave to all.

But I want you to notice that this is explicitly set in the context of the cross. Jesus gives his new teaching about authority after the audacious request of James and John to sit on his right and left hand. The equally ambitious remaining disciples are scandalized, and there is a row. But Jesus first answers the aspiring brothers in terms of the cup of suffering and the baptism of death that they too must share. And the punch-line of the whole story also anticipates the cross:

> The Son of Man came not to be served but to serve, and to give his life as a ransom for many.

Nor does this passage stand alone in the Gospels. Without offering a catena of proof-texts, I shall just mention perhaps the most powerful image of authority and service: the Johannine account of the foot-washing. Nor is it accidental that this is set on the eve of Jesus' crucifixion (John 13.1ff):

If I, then, your Lord and Master, have washed your feet, you also ought to wash one another's feet.

Look, too, at St Paul's letters, especially the opening chapters of the first Epistle to the Corinthians:

The foolishness of God is wiser than men, and the weakness of God is stronger than men (I Cor, 1.25)

The consistent witness of the New Testament points to three ingredients in the Christian understanding of authority. *First*, authority is seen as *vulnerable*. It is vulnerable because it is the authority of love and it exists for our freedom and fulfilment. *Second*, Christian authority is for service and not for domination. *Third*, because it is the authority of love it is capable of creating a common life, of gathering together the scattered children of God, of establishing and maintaining a communion of persons with God and with each other. All this borders on the obvious: to speak of Christian authority for service is, as I have said earlier, to border on the platitudinous. And yet what we know notionally we fail to practise both individually and institutionally.

Authority not power

I have spoken of the swings of the pendulum in our Western political and social understanding of authority. I have already suggested that the churches mirror these swings. The churches seem in danger of returning to fundamentalisms of Bible or tradition after the breakdown of the liberal consensus of the 1960s and the 1970s. This should not surprise us. In the history of politics, tyranny and dictatorship are often the children of anarchy. But Christians need not accept these stark polarities as the only alternatives. To stress a proper Christian distinction between authority and power may be a theological commonplace. But it is a distinction not yet much found in the market-place, and I now turn your attention to it.

We know the distinction between authority and power to be true in the most fundamental of human relationships. Take the example of parent and child. At the beginning, the child lives in untroubled acceptance of parental authority, from which it draws its security, its information, its values. But there comes a time when that child begins to assert its autonomy: 'Why should I do this, simply because you tell me?' On the parents' side there is also a danger of stamping feet: 'You will do as you're told or you will go to bed.' The parent may win, but at the terrible cost of exercising parental *power* because he or she has lost parental *authority*. Authority is rarely claimed or asserted until it is well on the way to being lost.

Another way of seeing the distinction between authority and power is to recognize that authority always properly refers to a moral relationship, freely bestowed and accepted, between free and rational agents. In contrast the concept of power often refers to merely physical and material mechanisms. Significantly we speak of the 'levers of power'. Of course, we can speak of human beings having power over their fellows, but this is to suggest enslavement, whether literal, psychological or political. A prisoner or hostage may be in the power of his captors, but it would be odd to speak of his being under their authority.

I want to suggest that the only alternative recipe to the oscillation between authoritarianism and libertarianism will be the painful rediscovery of a true Christian authority. Nicholas Lash has said that while we speak of 'a power vacuum' when social and political systems collapse, perhaps what we ought to be speaking of is 'an authority vacuum'.[4] The Christian contribution will be to see that the vacuum is filled by a rediscovery of true authority rather than the institutionalized power of a new conservatism or the individualized power of a defunct liberalism. We do not want to be in the position of the person out of whom the unclean spirit departed – only to find the vacuum filled by seven other spirits worse than the first (Matt. 12.43–45).

The goal of power

But to make the rediscovery of a true Christian authority, we will need to go further than simply drawing the distinction between power and service. As I suggested earlier, we need to pay careful attention to the goal of Christian authority. If the goal of Christian authority is to bring human beings into a mature relationship with God and their fellows, crude coercive power will actually be counter-productive – as any parent knows to his or her cost. What is true about the actual exercise of authority in terms of human and social relations also corresponds

4. Nicholas Lash, 'Authority of Impotence', unpublished sermon, Great St Mary's, Cambridge, 22 April 1979.

to Christ's new teaching about a vulnerable authority, an authority between autonomous persons: in a word, an authority of the cross.

Perhaps the proper formula here is not, as many people appear to think, 'Not power, but service.' The formula which we need is surely rather: 'Only such power as is necessary for an authority of service.' The exercise of power can only be justified in the interests of empowering Christian women and men to be what God wants them to be. Those to whom power is given have always to bear in mind the ultimate goal of the church which, as we have seen, is the communion of free men and women with God and with each other.

Perhaps I can illustrate my modest rehabilitation of a circumscribed exercise of power by two examples. I have already spoken of the authority of parents over children in showing the distinction between authority and power. There are occasions, especially before children reach maturity, when crude power is actually necessary. I physically prevent my child putting its hand into the fire – in spite of its admirable curiosity and fascination for the beauty of the flame. Later the child will recognize that this crude exercise of power was right and my authority as parent will be ultimately enhanced rather than eroded.

Or – to take an example closer to the bone – the bishop has the responsibility to maintain faith and charity in his diocese. This implies that occasionally he may need to discipline or even remove a priest from a parish by force of canon law. No one would deny the regrettable need for such machinery, however rarely (fortunately) it has to be exercised. True, the moral authority of the bishop over the priest may be eroded as far as that one priest is concerned. But the bishop has to think of the congregation, of the rest of the diocese and the wider church. Occasionally, even power may be an appropriate part of Christian authority. But that is so only as long as it serves the wider goals of the church, and is never exercised for its own sake or for the vain glory of the exerciser.

I have suggested that the characteristically Christian insight about authority must be seen in the cross of Jesus Christ. Here authority is displayed as vulnerable, is seen to be for service rather than dominion and as creative of true fellowship. Such authority is never to be equated with power, and only occasionally to be associated with it in the wider interests of communion in charity. I believe this summary does justice to the whole picture of Jesus in the New Testament where his personal authority is usually conveyed in the indicative mood – as in his parables of the Kingdom, where the Kingdom is 'like this' or 'like that', or his acted parables like the washing of the Disciples' feet. And sometimes it is exercised in the interrogative mood: 'Whose image or superscription is this?' or 'Who do you say that I am?' – questions to enhance people's maturity. Only rarely is his authority in the imperative mood: 'Go, sin no more.'

Two maps of authority

I will end by a tentative attempt at the superimposition of my secular and Christian maps of authority. In the secular world we see a violent swing of the pendulum away from the liberal certainties of twenty years ago. So it is within the Christian churches. We also see a strong resurgence of both political and religious fundamentalisms. But this kind of authority can only now be restored by authoritarianism. We recognize that what is really required is a new understanding of authority which does not have power at its heart, whether authoritarian or libertine: an authority which has community and communion as its goal.

I do not believe the correspondence between our two diagnostic maps is coincidental. It should not come as a surprise to Christians that the creation yearns for the pattern exhibited in the incarnation.

On the day of my enthronement, eight years ago, I preached from the Gospel of the day, the Annunciation: 'And the Angel said to Mary, "Jesus shall be great and shall be called the Son of the Most High, and the Lord shall give him the throne of his Father David." ' On that day I, too, was given a throne. So in my sermon I reminded myself and others that Jesus was also given a throne. He was given authority: but of what kind! I remembered that the church has often tried to take short cuts to authority, enforcing respect and obedience by worldly means and so obscuring the face of God. When I came to the throne of St Augustine I was reminded of the men of power who had sat there before me by the pikes from the Archbishop's private army, which now decorate the walls of Lambeth Palace as museum pieces. And I was reminded by them of the temptation to gain the church's ends by the world's means. That temptation is still with us – until we remember the words: 'But it shall not be so among you.'

So if we have anything to offer the world as new maps of authority are being drawn it will be because we have not only remembered this prohibition, but also lived by it.

– 3 –

An Anglican Response

Diagnosis is usually easier than cure, and so far I have been attempting to set a discussion of authority in its contemporary secular context and to look at the general Christian principle of authority in the light of the cross. Now I must make a specifically Anglican response. The use of the indefinite article in conjunction with the adjective 'Anglican' is deliberate. The definite article would be perilous, even when used by the Archbishop of Canterbury. Furthermore, it is uncharacteristic of Anglicanism to claim to have any faith and order other than that of the one holy catholic and apostolic church. So, our answer to the problem of authority is unlikely to consist of entirely different ingredients from other Christian churches. But, of course, the mix may be a bit different; and our recipe may have something to be said for it, as all the churches come together in the ecumenical movement to offer their gifts in mutuality.

I argued earlier that contemporary polarizations and controversies challenge Christians to come to terms with authority as an inescapable part of life and to ask what sort of authority the church must have to achieve its goals. I argued at some length that traditional authoritarianism, the more recent permissive liberal free-for-all, and the inevitable lurch back into neo-conservatism, were all mistaken ways of looking at authority, and that the churches have mirrored the swinging of the pendulum to and fro.

So it is not surprising that people should sometimes politicize us, since we so much mirror what is happening in secular life. For example, I have recently been criticized in a notorious article as a 'liberal elitist', and a friend of mine from the higher reaches of British politics sent me a card which said: 'When the authoritarian populace are set to inherit the earth we need every liberal elitist we can find to stand in their way.' But we must not be seduced.

Tension, freedom and division

You may see this mirroring in the recent history of the episcopal church. In the continent of North America one can easily see the effects of the swing among other Christian groupings: in the growth of the moral majority churches, or the agonizing polarities of the Roman Catholic church. It's important for us Anglicans to recognize these tensions within ourselves. This is no time to be scoring points off other churches while the world yearns for someone to speak with true authority and not as the scribes. The very fact of our Christian bewilderment over authority can in itself be a good thing. We are part of the problem. And the recognition of this fact means that we can the more securely contribute something more than theory.

I spoke earlier of a certain convergence between secular and Christian diagnosis of the problem of authority in the search for a new understanding of authority for service in the building up of community and communion. It is here that the vulnerable authority of the cross is seen as strength rather than weakness. Paradoxically love is more powerful than power. If love, not power, is to rule the world, there must be freedom, and freedom is very risky. We can sink as empires like the Roman Empire sank – all pleasure and self-seeking – or we can be raised up by sacrificial love.

So far I have said nothing which is not common to all Christians, and I have already said that this should not surprise us as Anglicans, for we have always claimed to have no faith or order other than that of the undivided church. But in fact we have always recognized division in the church by our non-exclusive insistence of only being a part of the church catholic. Regrettably, we have to recognize that in a divided Christendom there have to be denominations. But it is important that we never permanently canonize Anglicanism. Denominations – including our own Anglican Communion – are only provisional necessities because of the frailty of human nature and the failure of Christian charity.

Anglicanism as dialogue

In what I now go on to say about an Anglican understanding of authority, and about structures of authority within the Anglican Communion, we must not think of ourselves as possessing anything more than this provisional character.

Yet there are certain constant Anglican themes when authority is discussed. Even our insistence on not having peculiar and special characteristics and doctrines may itself be a defining mark. I am reminded of a comment by the seventeenth-century philosopher David Hume, who defined an Englishman as one who, unlike other races, has no national characteristics!

I want to characterize the Anglican tradition as essentially a continuing dialogue between gospel and church. I need to set out briefly what I mean by gospel.

God did not send his church into the world – he sent us his word, his call to us to recognize that it is his world – for all that means about the way we should treat it, the way we should behave in it, the good news of his love for it, the good news that the very nature and purpose of the creation, of the way things really are, is embodied for us in the man Jesus. Jesus is the good news that by him we can be forgiven for our misuse of the world and our refusal to acknowledge its maker, and that committing ourselves to him we have the possibility of restoration and new life as children of the God whose world this is and which he has reconciled to himself.

The church is that part of the world which has accepted the gospel addressed to all people and tries to live by it.

On the one hand, the Word of God is accepted as having a fundamental, binding character. On the other hand, the church is the community which not only receives the gospel but has the duty to interpret, proclaim and celebrate it in word and sacrament. For this there must be a duly commissioned ministry of oversight and discernment which is itself continuously subject to the gospel. What I call the dialogue between gospel and church can be traced in past Anglican discussion about scripture, tradition and reason or in the Lambeth Quadrilateral. This is the dialogue to which Stephen Sykes refers when he speaks of the dialectical nature of Anglican theology in which debate and even conflict are part of our Anglican understanding of authority. [1]

The Anglican trilogy

Let us explore what I mean by this dialogue in relation to the famous Anglican trilogy of scripture, tradition and reason. It is proper to ask how this trilogy now stands. Would it still service our faith as it did the faith of our forefathers?

(a) Reason

Take reason, once thought to be the property of humankind, common to all ages and cultures. It was concerned with the process of speaking truth and was held to be self-evidently valid. It has to be admitted that since the Holocaust and Hiroshima we cannot now return to this Olympian Renaissance view of reason. Nor to the nineteenth-century belief in the triumph of liberal and scientific progress. Nevertheless we may ask whether anti-rationalism has gone too far. Intellectual activity is seen by some as bourgeois objectivism, lacking commitment to the so-called real gospel issues, and it is regarded with some suspicion. Words like 'academic' and 'cerebral' have developed a pejorative sense, and a term like 'head-trip' reveals a new and dangerous perspective on intellectual activity.

1. Stephen Sykes, *The Integrity of Anglicanism*, Mowbray 1978, p. 88.

(b) Scripture

Perhaps it is this new feature of contemporary life that helps to explain the readiness of so many to accept a one-dimensional view of scripture and see it as a monochrome account of divine activity without colour, variety or discrimination. It has never been more necessary for Anglicans to hold fast to this trilogy, to think clearly about their faith and to worship God with all their minds.

The necessity to hold together, without merging, religious experience and confidence in rational processes is a necessity of our time. Otherwise the gospel cuts off the believer from the other worlds he or she must inhabit and confines itself to the sidelines of human discovery and experience.

The authority of scripture certainly appears also to be under fire, as phrases such as 'the crisis in biblical authority' reveal. I have no wish to diminish the very profound questions biblical criticism raises for all Christians, but they are more sharply felt by those who place their sole reliance upon scripture.

The authority of scripture often seems to suffer as much from its adherents as from its detractors. Frequently its authority is thought to lie in some supposed inerrancy or infallibility that the church does not claim for it, and to be impugned by the application of literary criticism. In fact I believe modern biblical study can be immensely stimulating, enriching the imagination, stirring the conscience and provoking new insights into the faith. We should rejoice in the wealth of variety of scripture, even admire its intractability and resistance to the systematisers. Some people have said 'No one was ever converted by biblical criticism'. That's not true. I'm an example of it because when I was a boy at school, and not very religiously inclined, my scripture teacher gave me a book to read, now out of date, called *The Four Gospels* by B. Streeter. I read it like a detective story, discovering how people's experience in Ephesus and Rome and Jerusalem and Antioch had produced four different stories about Jesus. It was intriguing stuff!

Nor should we ignore new aspects of biblical renewal which have a direct bearing on the question of authority. The base ecclesial communities emerging in Latin America and parts of South-East Asia are an example of this kind of renewal. Reading the Bible in context has for many people highlighted themes in the Bible which have been ignored in traditional teaching and preaching. So, the prophetic concern for justice and Jesus's interest in the poor have been brought to the attention of the world-wide church.

This way of reading the Bible, moreover, has brought about a new way of doing theology. This approach, sometimes called 'doing theology from below' takes Jesus among the crowds in Galilee as its point of departure for engagement with the concerns of the poor and margin-alized as a valid way of doing biblical theology. So, base communities also tell us something important about the dialogue between gospel and church.

(c) Tradition

Tradition, the third of our three pillars, is now recognized less grudgingly as an essential part of our understanding of the gospel. It is through tradition that we have fellowship with our own past and learn to recognize our own voice. Tradition is a community's language. If our faith is to be judged and corrected from anywhere beyond the individual Christian heart, it is to our tradition we naturally turn.

But if tradition is to become the living voice and experience of the church, we Anglicans need to think of it in less documentary terms than in the past. Of course there are the creeds and the writings of the Fathers. Yet where does tradition stop? Do we include, as I hope we do, the greatest scholastic writers, the Anglican divines of the sixteenth and seventeeth centuries, or the nineteenth-century evangelicals and tractarians? We must guard against the view that tradition stops at certain dates. This is a view unconsciously fostered by the arbitrary dates which terminate church history syllabuses in our universities and theological colleges.

In proposing a dynamic view of tradition, as the language of the community and its living voice in fellowship with the past, I am aware of the danger of simply indentifying tradition with the contemporary experience or fashion of the twentieth-century church. We do not want to go down the road of Pius IX who, in conversations before the definition of Papal infallibility, made the celebrated retort 'La tradizione son Io' 'I am the tradition'. But in spite of dangers I look forward to a more positive appreciation of tradition for Anglicans in the future.

So, the three pillars are not exactly as they were in Richard Hooker's day. Nevertheless, I hope I have shown that an appeal to them is still not to be despised. Their real strength, however, is their combination and relationship. There is a balance in this formula that continues to appeal

– part of what I call the dialogue between church and gospel – which I would suggest is characteristic of Anglicanism. In this dialogue there is a constant interplay between human reason, culture, experience and the once-for-all given revelation.

New ways for old truths

It is not enough simply to repeat the words of scripture. New ways must be found to expound old truths. The Nicene Creed itself is the product of this interplay between revelation and culture, which goes beyond the words of scripture and yet does so only to promote and protect the integrity of the original gospel.

Sometimes Anglicans feel the tensions of this exploration more than other Christians. We have had some recent debates in the Church of England over the nature of Christian belief in the Incarnation and Resurrection of Jesus Christ. And there been some vigorous debaters like the Bishop of Durham. But I am comforted by some words of an American Roman Catholic, the late Bishop Fulton Sheen, not himself a notable modernist. The story is told that when he was being questioned by journalists about a supposed split at Vatican II between conservatives and liberals he replied: 'These are political terms. In biblical terms there are two kinds of bishop: shepherds and fishermen. Shepherds care for the unity of the flock. Fishermen launch out adventurously into the deep. We need both!' Eventually the church will reach a common mind on issues, not easily or without controversy but steadily and surely. What was controverted opinion is tested and scrutinized and either rejected or eventually accepted as part of the continuing tradition of the church, in continuity with the past and in conformity with scripture, and yet indentical with neither. This is the dialogue between church and gospel.

This dialogue is not, however, between equal partners as in a civil contract. It is more like the covenantal relationship between God and his people. So, there is a primacy to the gospel which places everyone on the same level and standing before God. The gospel is accessible to everyone.

This does not mean an unbiblical fundamentalism. Nor does it mean a denial of the proper place of the church as 'the witness and the keeper of holy Writ'.[2]

Yet to insist that the church has a proper place in the interpretation and contemporary application of the gospel is not to believe in some form of continuous revelation, in which the scriptures no longer have relevance – an inference detectable in extreme forms of traditionalist catholicism and liberal modernism. The authority of the church is rather a 'showing forth', 'a proclaiming', of what has been 'once for all delivered to the saints' (Lambeth 1968). Or, in the words of a recent Church of England report, the church's pronouncements play a 'limited but creative role' in defining what is that faith which is uniquely revealed in the scriptures. [3]

But how is this interpretation on the part of the church to be done? As we have seen, and know ourselves, there are difficulties in scripture and past Christian tradition, and there are new challenges to be faced in the modern world where solutions are not easily read off the pages of

2. *Thirty-Nine Articles*, Article XX: 'Of the authority of the Church'.
3. *The Nature of Christian Belief*, p. 7.

the New Testament, the Fathers, or the *Book of Common Prayer*.

The office of the bishop

It is here that Anglican instinct has usually gone beyond the Reformation churches in recognizing the apostolic office of the bishop. It is emphatically *not* that the bishop has exclusive wisdom or inspiration. It is rather that Anglicans, following the example of the Christian centuries, have said that the president of word and sacrament in the local church is a personal focus for the preservation of the church's unity and faith and mission. It is he (I use the personal pronoun neutrally) who ordains and sends out priests into the mission field to proclaim the gospel of reconciliation in word and sacrament. The essential ministry of the bishop will be to keep the church true to the implications of the gospel in all its profundity, range and richness.

Anglicans believe that a ministry of oversight *(episcope)* is part of the Christian package of authority. What Anglicans see above all else within the historic episcopate is a ministry of oversight which promotes the unity in time and place of the church in apostolic succession. And for this Anglican ordinals have required of bishops diligence in the study of scripture, effectiveness in teaching, orthodoxy in doctrine, wholesomeness of life, and the tempering of justice with mercy in the administration of discipline.

Local and global

It will not, however, have escaped many today that, despite the possible attractiveness of an Anglican theology of dialogue between church and gospel, there is a serious gap in the Anglican tradition as I have sketched it so far. We have a both/and theology of authority: both the transcendent gospel affirming human equality – all have access to the gospel – *and* the human necessity for an authorized ministry. But thus far this is only at the local level of bishop, clergy and people in a diocese. Indeed, Anglican thinking about the unity within a province, a nation or at the ecumenical and global level was minimal before the sharp questions now raised by our ecumenical partners – not least Rome – and by our internal Anglican divisions over the ordination of women.

Some critics – including Anglicans – have called Anglicanism an episcopal or diocesan congregationalism. And there is just enough force in the jibe for us to need to take the criticism seriously. Of course a very strong sense of the local diocesan church is thoroughly patristic. Cyprian would have approved. It is also very much in accordance with the continued thinking of the Orthodox churches. Furthermore, if we take seriously the principle of doing nothing centrally which is more appropriately done at local level, as I was suggesting in a secular context, there may well be more to be said for Anglican provincial and diocesan autonomy than such critics allow.

Other critics have noticed our strong provincial structures even if we have not theologized about them very much. They have then gone on to ask why there are no juridical structures at a global level. Why is unity only focussed personally at a local level, through the bishops, or expressed juridically at a provincial level? The answer lies not so much in Anglican ecclesiology as in Anglican history.

A matter of history

The historic reason for the shape of Anglicanism is plain
enough, namely the refusal to admit the authority and
power of the Pope within the realms of Henry VIII, and
only then the subsequent theological justification of the
idea of a national Church. Ecumenical unity was, it was
supposed in the sixteenth century, only likely to be
restored by a General Council; moreover one called 'by
the commandment and will of Princes' (Article XXI).

But just as the historical crises of faith were the cause
for the need to develop structures within the early church,
notably ecumenical councils and the enlarged exercise of
episcopal influence that we call primacy, so Anglicanism
in the last two hundred years had also developed. And
we need to reflect with some theological rigour upon this
development.

I do not believe the development of the autonomous
provinces of the Anglican Communion to be unprovidential. But nor do I believe the development of Anglican
episcopal collegiality in the first Lambeth Conference of
1868 to have been without the promptings of the Spirit.
And it has been from the calling of the Lambeth Conferences that the role of the Archbishop of Canterbury as a
focus of loyalty for the Communion has also developed.

Dispersed authority

Since then, other organs of authority, such as the Anglican
Consultative Council and the Primates' Meeting, have
arisen according to particular needs and requirements of
a developing world communion. As Anglicans have
begun to reflect upon the different levels and sources of

authority within the Communion, the notion of *dispersed authority* has resonated as the proper way of describing the unique combination of elements which go to make up the decision-making which we have.

The best description of this is still perhaps that of the 1948 Lambeth Conference:

> Authority is distributed among Scripture, Tradition, Creeds, the Ministry of the Word and Sacraments, the witness of Saints, and the *consensus fidelium*, which is the continuing experience of the Holy Spirit through His faithful people in the Church. It is thus a dispersed rather than a centralised authority having many elements which combine, interact and check each other.

Even if we are not so clear-cut as other churches in our Christian understanding of authority, whether 'biblical', 'confessional' or 'magisterial', it will be clear enough that the Lambeth 1948 description of Anglican dispersed authority is yet another way of talking about the dialogue between gospel and church.

But awkward questions need to be faced, we know of countless examples in church history of the capacity of churches to redescribe their own history in ideological terms. It was that good Anglican, Bishop Butler, who dryly observed:

> We are exceedingly prone to deceive ourselves, and judge too favourably on every aspect, where ourselves and our own interests are concerned.

The principle of a dialogue between gospel and church must result in a proper self-criticism of our structures and understanding of authority. Such self-criticism will inevitably need to look at the goal of Christian authority which I outlined – communion between humanity and God and between each other. We need to set all our structures against this yardstick to see if they are lacking.

I believe that it is significant that we Anglicans describe ourselves as a Communion. We rejoice in this, but we must not imagine that we need do nothing to maintain communion. Relationships need time, care and above all love if they are to flourish and develop. When strains arise, say in a marriage, the institution of marriage itself gives space and freedom for healing, for self-restraint, for restoring communion between husband and wife.

The ordination of women

No one will question that it has been the contentious issue of the ordination of women to the priesthood (and now episcopate) which has demonstrated an inadequacy in the central structures of the Anglican Communion.

The structures themselves – Lambeth Conference, Consultative Council, Primates' Meeting – are not to blame. For the question of whether the ordination of women is a genuine development of authentic Christian tradition is notoriously difficult to answer decisively in a divided Christendom. And until there is a decisive, ecumenical, Christian answer to this question there will inevitably be the risk of broken, or at least impaired, communion between the provinces of our Communion, where some have advanced while others have held back. This is not so much because the ordination of women, or non-ordination of women, is itself a fundamental question at the heart of the faith – it is clearly not as central to faith as, say, the doctrines of the Incarnation or the Holy Trinity. But differing actions on this matter (as opposed to varied opinions) do threaten communion because the ordained ministry, and especially the episcopate, is the instrument of communion.

We should have known this all along. For was it not, after all, Anglicans like Bishop Charles Brent who tirelessly insisted in the beginnings of the Ecumenical Movement that faith and order go together. They are not of equal importance, but apostolic order is the means of maintaining the unity in diversity of the church's life.

Strengthening the structures for Communion

So, we are beginning to hear calls for a strengthening of the structures of world Anglicanism. Exploration began at the meeting of the Anglican Consultative Council in Singapore in April last year. The Lambeth Conference, the Anglican Consultative Council, the Primates and my own office all need to be examined if we are to strengthen the bonds which hold us together. Even the shibboleth of provincial independence will need to be scrutinized – though the Church of England would be as resistant as any of the more liberal of Anglican provinces to any infringement of its self-conscious sovereignty.

It was the late and lamented Dr Gareth Bennett, the author of the recent unhappy *Crockford's* Preface, who surprisingly became a champion of a reconstituted Consultative Council. In a passage he clearly felt very deeply about – more deeply perhaps than his supposed attack on myself he wrote:

It seems probable that there will have to be some self-denying ordinance by which the provinces agree that certain matters shall not be decided locally but only after a common mind has been established among the Churches. Finding a constitution for a new kind of Council will not be easy, but it is perhaps not too much to say that the future of Anglicanism as a world Christian community depends on its being achieved.

All this is for discussion and debate. Such matters will figure prominently in the forthcoming Lambeth Conference, where questions of authority will again be highly prominent.

At the Lambeth Conference the authority agenda will not only be set by internal Anglican affairs but also by our ecumenical partners. I think here especially of the final report of the Anglican Roman Catholic International Commission and its radical proposals for a renewed and reformed universal primacy to give visible expression to unity at the global level.

Consent of the faithful

All this discussion about the adequacy or otherwise of the existing Anglican structures must not, however, detract us from a final but crucial aspect of our consideration of the dialogue between gospel and church. We have seen that a dispersed notion of authority has been characteristic of Anglicanism. This is essentially a combination of different sources, aspects and levels of authority. In England in the sixteenth century there was a distribution between four major agents of authority: the sovereign, the parliament, the bishops and synods. In Anglicanism overseas the laity were given a constitutional place from the beginning of the autonomy of churches such as that of the United States or New Zealand.

Why should this have been so? In all probability the inclusion of a role for Parliament in Henry VIII's plans for his headship of the church was an accident in the development of English politics. But the constitutional result was the *consent* of the people which it represented. And that is also an essential theological point of some importance within Anglicanism.

Everyone has access to the gospel. This is not to say that ecclesiastical democracy easily equals the *consensus fidelium*. Those of us who know the politics of a synod and the difficulties of electing representative lay people, not mere tokens, will not lightly equate a bare majority in a church council with the voice of the people of God. But the development of an institutional voice for the laity appears to be a significant contribution of Anglicanism. We must learn from our mistakes, as well as from the experience of other churches. We must also recognize that this development may be something we have to bring to other episcopal churches. The bishop in synod is the product of our experience, our modern Anglican tradition.

In the end all instruments of authority of the church must share the frailty and fallibility of human institutions. So, Anglicans – along with all other Christians – have recognized that General Councils may, and sometimes have, erred. And with councils also popes, primates and bishops, synods and conventions. The *consensus fidelium* is not about correct procedures or the external credentials of authoritative persons or institutions. It is rather about that complex theological question of how the whole church 'receives' the decisions of bishops, councils, and synods.

This is not a matter of the laity having a simple veto. To think of the laity separately from the clergy and bishops is just as dangerous as thinking of the clergy and the bishops without the laity. The whole church is the *laos*. The unordained part of the people of God have a pro-active role in testing, scrutinizing and proposing how the faith must be proclaimed to those who have the ministry of listening and speaking on behalf of the church. The ordained ministry is commissioned to discern and articulate the word of God. The dialogue between gospel and church finds its expression in this ministry of the word.

In the end – but not usually quickly – God's Spirit will show the whole church whether such a decision or development had its origin in the same Spirit or not. There are no short cuts, no easy ways. I speak as a modest historian of the early church. I value the Lambeth 1948 description of the *consensus fidelium* as 'the *continuing experience* of the Holy Spirit'.

The Gamaliel principle

The Anglican Communion is in the middle of a major debate about authority in relation to the ordination of women. In the end the Gamaliel principle is the true Christian response. If a thing is of God it will flourish – if not it will eventually wither. In the meantime we have to endure the pain felt by protagonists and antagonists alike – that is the cost of the dialogue between church and gospel.

Why make it all so difficult? Why not just do a thing if

it seems right and damn the rest – or don't do it and damn those who do? There have been too many anathemas in church history and often because of a simplistic longing for certainties that are not to be had. Do not blame theologians or archbishops for the complexities of the map of authority! You expect a cartographer to draw a map with some semblance to the geographical configuration it represents. Over-simplified maps are the surest ways of getting lost.

Over-detailed maps, on the other hand, can only be read by those trained in map reading. So in drawing this Anglican response to its conclusion I am aware of the need to offer a broad picture on the question of authority as I see it. I have characterized the Anglican response in terms of a dialogue between gospel and church. I have worked this out in some detail in relation to the venerable Anglican trilogy of scripture, tradition and reason.

I have spoken of some of the implications of the primacy of the gospel and also of the need for an authoritative human response in the ministry of the word and sacrament which for Anglicans is focussed in the historic episcopate. Not for nothing are Anglicans also called episcopalians.

I then reminded you of some questions facing Anglicans today in relation to changes and developments within the ordained ministry and asked whether they can be appropriately decided at provincial level without threatening communion.

Finally, I turned to the question of how decisions are not only made but also received in the universal church. Here we see again the role of primates, bishops, clergy and laity; the continuing experience of the Holy Spirit within the whole church, that is the *consensus fidelium*, a phrase I sometimes like to translate as the common sense of the people of God.

The role of worship

How can all this be seen together as a piece? I have not yet spoken about worship. Yet some observers of Anglicanism would see our ordered pattern of biblical and credal worship as a major constituent of the Anglican understanding of authority – *lex orandi, lex credendi* – the law of praying is the law of believing.

It was already mentioned in the Lambeth 1948 description of dispersed authority. I raise it now not because I believe it to be less important than other elements we have already examined, but because it is within Anglican liturgical worship that they all cohere.

The paradigm for Christian worship is the celebration of the eucharist, presided over by the bishop, assisted by presbyters and deacons, and in association with the whole congregation of the people of God. In such a celebration of the eucharist the story of the life, death and resurrection of Jesus Christ is proclaimed through the reading of the word. The present and past teaching of the church is expounded through the sermon and the corporate recitation of the creed. The inner life of grace is renewed by the sacramental remembrance of Christ's presence and sacrifice, and this is effected through the unworthy ministrations of the chief shepherd, the bishop, who is also the link person between this celebration of the eucharist and the rest of the church universal in time and space. That is the meaning of the apostolic succession.

To end with worship is no pious peroration. Authentic

Christian worship always points us out into the world. The conclusion of the eucharist literally directs us back to where we have come from. Worship is not escapism. Augustine taught us that we receive the eucharistic body of Christ only in order to become the body of Christ in the world.

From the church to the world

I have necessarily spent some time talking about ecclesiastical matters. But it would be a disastrously limited vision if I suggested that the ecclesiastical is the be-all and end-all. In a powerful address to the Anglican Consultative Council in Singapore, Nicholas Lash warned Anglicans of the dangers of an ecclesiastically-centred discussion of authority. We should heed his warning. The structures of Christian authority may not in the end be considered apart from the unity, redemption and reconciliation of the whole human race. For the church exists not for itself but for others. It exists for the sake of the kingdom of God of which it is herald, foretaste, instrument, sign and sacrament – to use the language Anglicans have used with Reformed and Roman Catholic ecumenical partners.

Because the church must never forget that the kingdom comes first, must never forget that the gospel which I outlined to you comes first, my discussion must rightly begin and end in the world. As Professor Lash put it:

It is only where people actually bleed and weep that their wounds can be bound up and their tears wiped away.

If we Anglicans are wounded and shed some tears in the debate about authority that is no bad thing. We must not expect anything different from the Lord of the church whose glory was the cross. And only if we have wept and bled ourselves will be able to say something constructive about authority in the wider secular world.

I spoke earlier of an authoritative service. I have gone on to talk about an Anglican dialogue between gospel and church in which such an authority must be exemplified. But in both it is a matter of recognizing the authority of Jesus Christ. I do not think that the world is so far from wanting to recognize such authority. Let me therefore end with a secular text, though one of some antiquity and profundity and simplicity: the gospel is accessible for all. It comes from Shakespeare's *King Lear*. The Earl of Kent comes to offer his service to King Lear, and the following dialogue ensues:

L: What wouldst thou?
K: Service.
L: Who wouldst thou serve?
K: You.
L: Dost thou know me, fellow?
K: No Sir, but you have that in your countenance which I would feign call Master.
L: What's that?
K: Authority.

The world does not know Jesus Christ, but I believe it is prepared to recognize in his countenance that which it would feign call Master, and to say with those who met with him long ago: 'He spoke with authority.'